The Theatre Arts
Audition
Book for Women

The Theatre Arts
Audition
Book for Women

Compiled by Annika Bluhm

A Theatre Arts Book
Routledge • New York

Published in the USA and Canada in 2003 by
Routledge
29 West 35th Street
New York, NY 10001
www.routldge-ny.com

Routledge is an imprint of the Taylor & Francis Group

First printed in Great Britain in 1989 by Methuen Drama
This revised and updated edition first published in 2003 by
Methuen Publishing Limited
215 Vauxhall Bridge Road
London SW1V 1EJ

Printed in the United States of America on acid-free paper.

10 9 8 7 6 5 4 3 2 1

Library of Congress Cataloging-in-Publication Data
The theatre arts audition book for women / compiled by Annika Bluhm.
    p. cm.
    ISBN 0-87830-173-9 (alk. paper)
    1. Acting. 2. Auditions. 3. English drama—20th century. 4. American drama—20th century. 5. Women—Drama. I. Bluhm, Annika.

PN2080.T49 2003
812'.50809287—dc21   2002036914

Contents

Thank you to Andrew, Griffin and Arden Farrow.

Introduction

In the course of compiling this book I spoke to a number of directors working in various areas of theatre, from drama schools to the National Theatre. Nearly everyone agreed that an actor's most important attribute was self-knowledge. Self-knowledge can be expressed in a variety of ways: through wit, intelligence, verbal and physical dexterity, an assertive, as opposed to an aggressive manner.

There is a great difference in approach to auditioning in Britain and the United States. In America cut-throat competition has engendered a highly professional attitude. Actors tend to arrive fully prepared for an audition, on time, with well-rehearsed speeches from plays that they have taken the time to read in their entirety. In contrast directors spoke about the appalling diffidence of many actors in Britain, who arrived in no way prepared, appearing to feel that the audition was something of an imposition and that performing was the last thing in the world they wanted to do.

Directors were keen to emphasize the fact that an audition is not a test but a meeting between the actor and director to assess the possibility of working together. Many felt that auditioning should be more of a two-way process and that actors should accept more power or responsibility for themselves when auditioning. In other words, actors should not be tempted to play down their own intelligence, to act according to what they think the director wants, but to see themselves as professionals.

Opinions differ as to how much an actor can show about the way he/she works in an audition. One felt that it was a genuine opportunity for an actor to display their work; another, that little could actually be revealed by the presentation of a speech – auditioning being an artificial performing situation – and that the actor should concentrate on presenting *themselves* as well as possible, on maximizing their presence. Clearly in an ideal audition one should do both. One should be clear, concise and, equally important, unpretentious. One director talked of avoiding the

1

temptation to be arch. Another was looking for 'assurance with natural reticence', which she went on to explain as including the director in the audition in an open way, talking with, rather than at, him or her.

Most key points as regards the selection and presentation of the audition piece are common sense, but easy to overlook in the attempt to impress. For instance it would be unwise to attempt a speech using a particular accent unless it was well within your capabilities and it would be sensible to choose a role within your own age-range. In the event of an audition being for a specific role, select a pertinent piece: if the production is to be a comedy, present a comic speech. It should be emphasized that there is no substitute, when preparing an audition speech, for reading the play in its entirety.

Everybody acknowledged the advantages of doing a witty or comic piece mainly because they enjoyed being able to laugh. They felt that it was extremely hard for an actor to play a highly emotional scene in an audition without resorting to a good deal of tension, both physically and vocally.

How can you make auditioning a less nerve-racking affair? Most directors agreed on this. Get a good night's sleep, wear comfortable clothes, arrive early and find a quiet place to calm down and 'centre' yourself. Above all, everyone stressed, *have fun*!

Some speeches are amalgamated. This is indicated by punctuation: [. . .].

After Miss Julie *by Patrick Marber*

It is the night of the Labour landslide victory of 1945. Miss Julie, the highly-strung daughter of a Labour peer, is left behind with the servants while her father goes to London to celebrate. Miss Julie has got drunk at the celebrations and finally succumbed to the on-going sexual flirtation between herself and the family chauffeur, John. At this point in the play Miss Julie has slept with John for the first time, losing her virginity in the process. The two find themselves caught in a passionate and destructive relationship with each alternately humiliating the other. Having explained that her father, despite his Labour background, would never accept a cross-class relationship between herself and John, she tells him about her parents' relationship.

Julie Did I tell you about my mother? She was quite common, you know . . . she had this thing about women's emancipation . . . she swore she'd never marry so she told my father she would be his lover but never his wife. But then, I was born, I was . . . a mistake really – . . . So they got married and my mother brought me up as . . . a child of nature, she used me to demonstrate the equality of sexes. She used to dress me up in boy's clothes and made me learn about farming – she made me kill a fox when I was – and then she reorganised the estate, the women had to do the men's work and the men the women's. We were the laughing stock of the whole county. Finally my father snapped and she fell in line. But she began to stay out all night . . . she took lovers, people talked, she blamed my father for the failure of her brave new world . . . her infidelities were her revenge. They rowed constantly, and fought, she often had terrible gashes and bruises . . . he did too, she was very strong when she was angry . . . and then there was a rumour that my father tried to kill himself – [. . .] he failed . . . (*Smiling.*) . . . obviously. I didn't know whose side I was on . . . maybe I learnt all my emotions by the age of ten and never developed any more . . . a child experiences the world so deeply . . . without the sophistication to protect itself . . . it's not fair really.

Pause.

Anyway, my mother almost on her death-bed . . . no, on her death-bed, made me swear that I'd never be a slave to any man.

Donkey's Years *by Michael Frayn*

A group of university graduates return to their old halls for a college reunion. They are now all highly respected members of the Establishment. As the evening commences they gradually revert to their student personas – revealing how misconceived were their notions of themselves and each other. Lady Driver, now the Master's wife, was married to Roddy who is absent from the reunion. However, Lady Driver is unaware of this fact as she confronts the man whom she believes to be Roddy in his darkened room.

Lady Driver Brown corduroy trousers. I'd forgotten your brown corduroy trousers. They can't be the same brown corduroy trousers you were wearing that weekend we stayed at the Ritz . . . (*Starting to cry.*)

I'm sorry, Roddy. I can't help it. It's the trousers. It's just suddenly coming face to face with your brown corduroy trousers in there when I'd forgotten about them. Thrown down all over the floor with no legs inside them . . . Just don't say anything. And don't look at me. If you just leave me alone for a minute I'll be alright . . . I didn't plan this, of course, I didn't plan to walk in after 17 years and burst into tears. It was just seeing the trousers half on the bed and half off, and one sock on the washstand . . . It was just having to wait in the bedroom while everyone was shouting in here . . . I didn't plan to be in the bedroom, of course. It didn't occur to me that you might bring back some horde of people here after dinner. Didn't you think I might be here? Didn't it cross your mind that I might be waiting somewhere? Or have you just completely forgotten about me . . .? Look I'm not crying because of you. I didn't come to have some terrible nostalgic scene, because I don't feel like that about it. I never think about the past. I'm far too busy with the present. I lead a very active life. I just came to see how you were and

6

to tell you how I was, and I'm fine, I'm very happy, things have turned out very well for me, and all I'm crying about is that I have to stand and tell you all this while I'm crying . . . The sound of you jumping to wrong conclusions is deafening. . . . Now you won't even look at me. You won't say anything. One of your famous silences. That's why everyone was always so impressed by you – because you just stood there and grinned and said nothing . . . I'm not angry about what happened. I can see it was my fault. But I wasn't really going to walk out! I came back to the hotel that night and you'd gone. I know I *said* I was going to walk out. But you hadn't said a word all the way from Tripoli to Tunis! Somebody had to say something! I know I took all the money – but that was so you couldn't leave. It's just that I met these people I knew, and I went to have a drink with them, and so on, and so forth, and when I got back you'd gone, and all the rest of it, and obviously the postcard I sent to explain about everything only got to you after the engagement had been announced in *The Times* . . . Anyway I've changed. I've become very punctilious among other things. Perhaps because of the mistake I made with you. You may not believe this, but I often think about what happened. I often think about you. . . . Oh God, I shouldn't have come. I see now, it's disastrous. The whole plan's gone wrong.

Treehouses *by Elizabeth Kuti*

Eva, newly orphaned, remembers her loving but acrimonious relationship with her dead father. Throughout the play it becomes clear that Eva and her father carry the memory of various secrets and betrayals.

At this point in the play Eva's father has just died and she's preparing to give the oration at his funeral.

———————

Eva It's the little things of course always the little things that get you unguarded moments which survive for some mysterious reason just snapshots a boring day a trivial act bringing crisps and orange juice out from a pub to you in a car park or a tired look on his face one night trying to make the video work or some terrible joke he made and found hilarious just sitting on the grass in summer with a beer and the day was full of bees and pollen little things little things make it real make his death so so

As **Eva** *speaks light comes up on* **Young Magda** *kissing the* **Boy** *on the mouth.*

and then there's all the packing and the sorting and the cards and the flowers and all the best clothes and what do you wear on this day this day which promises to be hot you can see it from the haze the grass is wet and smells sweet smells of summer death in the summer the birds still sing that's what they say isn't it the birds still sing fuck them the world still so beautiful full of pleasures full of full so strange the way you're on this rollercoaster one minute all fine ringing the caterers grown up and will there be sausage rolls yes please and wine and jelly and why not must eat must drink it's what you do and then next minute there's that time when you said some bitch of a thing some hateful thing and he poured whisky in his glass and laughed that horrible laugh he did when he was hurt and it's like dad I'm sorry I don't know why I sorry I'm sorry but

Eva *consults her notepad.*

I would like to say a few words about my father

I would like to say a few words

9

Joyriders *by Christina Reid*

Joyriders is set in Belfast, where a group of young offenders are taking part in a government Youth Opportunities Programme. The aim of the scheme is to provide them with 'helpful' skills enabling them to find employment at the end of the year.

Maureen is sweet, naïve – and innocent. She lives alone with her younger brother Johnny, a habitual glue-sniffer and joy-rider. Maureen is pregnant by a university student, a fact she has kept secret from everyone but her friend Sandra.

Sandra has just left the room, taunting Maureen with the prospect of swollen ankles now that she is pregnant. Maureen responds by half-answering Sandra and half-talking to her unborn child.

———————————

Maureen There's nuthin' the matter with my ankles . . .

She begins to work the knitting machine, stops, looks down.

Don't heed her baby . . . he loves me . . . I know he does . . . he said he did . . . and he's a gentleman . . .

She operates the knitting machine again, stops.

We're gonna live in an old house behind the university . . . and every day I'll put you in your pram and wheel you round the Botanic Gardens . . . a proper pram . . . Silver Cross with big high wheels . . . and everybody'll look at you, you'll be that beautiful . . . your father's dark eyes an' your granny's blonde hair . . .

She stops at the thought of her mother. **Sandra** *comes in, sets the milk down, watches and listens to* **Maureen** *who doesn't see her.*

Your granny was like the sun . . . all golden . . . she lit up everything she touched . . . she come from the country and got cooped up in the flats like a battery hen . . . the day your granda went to England to look for work, we were that miserable she took me an' Johnnie to the pictures . . . The Wizard of Oz . . . it was lovely . . . an' the next day she bought seven pot plants . . . seven . . . an' she put them in a row on the kitchen window sill an' she said . . . 'They'll all flower except for the fourth one. That one has to stay green.' And she wouldn't tell us why. 'Wait and see' she said . . . 'Wait and see.' We watched an' we waited for a while an' nuthin happened, an' we lost interest. Didn't even notice them any more. And then one day I come in from school an' all the pot plants had flowers except the fourth one, just like she said.

She smiles and counts on her fingers.

Red, orange, yellow, green, blue, indigo, violet . . . 'See' she said, 'we have a rainbow on our window sill.'

See looks round, sees **Sandra**.

You come in that day . . . do you remember?

Cooking with Elvis *by Lee Hall*

Jill's father, an Elvis impersonator, has been paralysed in a crash. His fourteen-year-old daughter, Jill, and his wife both try to deal with their grief in different ways. Jill, who sees herself as fat, unpopular and unattractive, tries to divert her feelings about her father and his loss into her cooking.

In this speech Jill explains how she was told about her father's accident.

Jill I was standing there with a spatula when they said you were dead.

Lights up. Jill is standing with a wok. She adds oil.

There was some linguine and a jar full of capers and some nice marinaded olives and they were going on about tubes and intensive care and what a terrible shame it was et cetera. And then they brought in Mam and we went downstairs and all her mascara had run and she was moaning on and everything and I said she better hurry up or the pasta would be boiled to a glue. And then she started shaking and that, and I was in my apron, and then she told me, that in fact there'd been a miracle, and in fact you weren't dead and somehow you'd pulled through. And thought sod the linguine and started to cry.

She has been cooking furiously throughout the speech. She adds more ingredients. And towards the end of the speech she flambés the contents of the wok.

And there at that point something changed deep inside me. Something changed that was good. You see, in my whole life up until that point, in my whole life, I was the one who was always left out, I was the one stuck in my bedroom, I was the one nobody fancied, I was the one they always called fatty, I was the one with the hideous hairband, I was the one who couldn't stop burping, always in her shadow, always the one without a clue. But suddenly, in that special moment, everything became clear and I saw a reason, a purpose, a mission, like a beacon in the darkness, a guiding star in the night, and I just looked at them through the pain and the tears and the anguish and I said: 'Take me back to domestic science.'

Fear and Misery In The Third Reich *by*
Bertolt Brecht

Fear and Misery . . . is a series of short scenes showing how all strata of society in Germany were affected by the mistrust and violence bred by the Nazi regime.

A Jewish wife, married to a gentile doctor in Germany in the 1930s, is preparing to flee from the growing Nazi persecution. Before her husband arrives home from work she rehearses to herself how she will break the news of her departure to him.

———————————

Jewish Wife Yes, I'm packing. Don't pretend you haven't noticed anything the last few days. Nothing really matters, Fritz, except just one thing: if we spend our last hour together without looking at each other's eyes. That's a triumph they can't be allowed, the liars who force everyone else to lie. Ten years ago when somebody said no one would think I was Jewish, you instantly said yes, they would. And that's fine. That was straightforward. Why take things in a roundabout way now? I'm packing so they shan't take away your job as senior physician. And because they've stopped saying good morning to you at the clinic, and because you're not sleeping nowadays. I don't want you to tell me I mustn't go. And I'm hurrying because I don't want to hear you telling me I must. It's a matter of time. Principles are a matter of time. They don't last for ever, any more than a glove does. (There are good ones which last a long while. But even they only have a certain life.) Don't get the idea that I'm angry. Yes, I am. Why should I always be understanding? What's wrong with the shape of my nose and the colour of my hair? I'm to leave the town where I was born just so they don't have to go short of butter. What sort of people are you, yourself included? You work out the quantum theory and the Trendelenburg test, then allow a lot of semi-barbarians to tell you you're to conquer the world but you can't have the woman you want. The artificial lung, and the dive-bomber! You are monsters or you pander to monsters. Yes, I know I'm being unreasonable, but what good is reason in a world like this? There you sit watching your wife pack and saying nothing.

Two *by Ron Elisha*

The play is set in Germany shortly after the creation of the state of Israel. A young Jewish woman comes to a Rabbi for Hebrew lessons. She is secretive about her past and over the course of the lessons the Rabbi comes to realise that she is actually an SS officer from the death camps who is trying to hide and start a new life outside Germany.

In the following speech Anna describes her own past revealing that she is actually Jewish and is full of self-loathing for her own part in the war.

———————————

Anna   He . . . loved her . . . It was only later that he found out she was Jewish. Too late, for him . . . He forced her to convert. But then, when Hitler came to power, that wasn't enough. He found himself trapped, between his love and his hatred. But he didn't turn her in, that wasn't his style. He chose, instead, to start a new life. New job, new city, new papers, new name. Everything new. Except his wife. From that day on, he lived in fear of his life. And he made her pay for that fear. With a thousand and one humiliations. She was like a prisoner, with nowhere else to go. He used to beat her. Used to make her sleep in the kitchen. After a while, he couldn't even look at her, and she was barred from entering our part of the house . . . I watched her change, over the years, from a proud and beautiful woman to a miserable . . . scraping animal. In the beginning, he used to force me to curse her as she knelt, scrubbing the floors. After a while, he didn't have to force. I hated her. I hated everything about her. She was no longer human . . . I hated her because she had allowed herself to be turned into a pitiful, grovelling . . . nothing. Because she was a Jew. And I was a Jew. And when I looked at her I saw myself. And I hated her for it . . . One day, he beat her very badly, and broke her arm. That night, she took me aside and told me she was going to stay with relatives who were in hiding in Berlin. She kissed me. I wiped my cheek. That was the last time I ever saw her. Years later, I heard she'd been lost in an air raid. She died a Jew . . . After she left, I heard my father crying. I'd never heard a man cry like that before. I went in to him. He didn't want me there. I persisted and he slapped my face. I knew then that I, too, had to go . . . A year later, I was in the SS. Oh, my God. He was my father . . . He made me hate my mother. He made me hate myself. With so much hate inside me, there was nowhere else to go. I wanted to kill. To rid myself, once and for all, of that pitiful shadow . . . Oh, my God . . . my God . . . (*Crying.*) She kissed me . . . She kissed me and I wiped my cheek.

Educating Rita *by Willy Russell*

Educating Rita is a two-hander following the relationship between Rita, a bright Liverpudlian hairdresser, and her Open University English professor, Frank. As the course progresses Rita's passion to find herself a 'better life' has a profound effect upon the world-weary tutor.

In this speech Rita attempts to explain to Frank why she felt unable to come to a party at his home.

Rita (*angrily*) But I don't wanna be charming and delightful: funny. What's funny? I don't wanna be funny. I wanna talk seriously with the rest of you, I don't wanna spend the night takin' the piss, comin' on with the funnies because that's the only way I can get into the conversation. I didn't want to come to your house just to play the court jester. (. . .)

But I don't want to be myself. Me? What's me? Some stupid woman who gives us all a laugh because she thinks she can learn, because she thinks that one day she'll be like the rest of them, talking seriously, confidently, with knowledge, livin' a civilized life. Well, she can't be like that really but bring her in because she's good for a laugh!

I'm all right with you, here in this room; but when I saw those people you were with I couldn't come in. I would have seized up. Because I'm a freak. I can't talk to the people I live with anymore. An' I can't talk to the likes of them on Saturday, or them out there, because I can't learn the language. I'm a half-caste. I went back to the pub where Denny was, an' me mother, an' our Sandra, an' her mates. I'd decided I wasn't comin' here again. I went into the pub an' they were singin', all of them singin' some song they'd learnt from the juke-box. An' I stood in that pub an' thought, just what the frig am I trying to do? Why don't I just pack it in an' stay with them, an' join in the singin'?

(*Angrily.*) You think I can, don't you? Just because you pass a pub doorway an' hear the singin' you think we're all O.K., that we're all survivin', with the spirit intact. Well I did join in with the singin', I didn't ask any questions, I just went along with it. But when I looked round me mother had stopped singin', an' she was cryin', but no one could get it out of her why she was cryin'. Everyone just said she was pissed an' we should get her home. So we did, an' on the way I asked her why. I said, 'Why are y' cryin', Mother?' She said, 'Because – because we could sing better songs than those.' Ten minutes later, Denny had her laughing and singing again, pretending she hadn't said it. But she had. And that's why I came back. And that's why I'm staying.

Junk *by John Retallack, adapted from the novel by Melvin Burgess*

Fourteen-year-old Gemma, eager to escape the strictures of her suburban home, runs away with her boyfriend Tar. The two of them are soon involved in the drugs scene and the pay follows their inevitable decline into addiction, prostitution and crime.

In this scene Gemma explains the basic 'how to' rules of running away successfully.

————————————

Gemma (*to audience*) Well, here it is – what you've all been waiting for, Gemma Brogan's practical handbook to running away from home. A step-by-step guide:

One. You will need: Clothes – woolly vest, plenty of keep-warm stuff. Plenty of underwear and other personal items. A waterproof coat. A personal stereo. A sleeping bag. A pencil and paper. Money. Your father's bank card and PIN number.

Two. Your wits. You'll need 'em.

Three. Think about it. What are your mum and dad going to do? Try to get you back of course. It'll be police. It'll be, oh, my God, my little girl has been abducted. It'll be, maybe some dreadful pervert is at her right now. Maybe she's lying murdered in a bin liner in the town rubbish tip THIS VERY SECOND! It never occurs to them that little Lucinda got so fed up with Mumsy and Dadsy that she actually left of her own accord. So . . . if you don't want every copper in the land on your tail and pictures of you shining out of all the national newspapers, you tell your mum and dad *exactly* what you're doing.

Four. This is where the pencil and paper comes in. You write them a note explaining that you're going away. Wish them luck, tell them no hard feelings and that you hope they will understand.

Five. Book your coach ticket using your father's Visa card.

Six. Go to the cash machine – take the money – and run.

Thank you very much.

Bazaar & Rummage *by Sue Townsend*

Katrina is one of three agoraphobic women who has been persuaded to take part in a jumble sale outside her home. She used to be a singer but now lives a sheltered life, completely protected by her overbearing husband Maurice. Katrina is conscious of her own good looks and has a sharp tongue towards the other women who are less 'feminine' in the accepted sense. In this speech she is describing her day to the trainee social worker, Fliss.

Katrina Well at eight o'clock Maurice brings me my breakfast on a tray. I have half a grapefruit, a soft-boiled egg, toast soldiers, a cup of tea and a five-milligram Librium. Then when he's gone to work I listen to Terry Wogan. He sometimes plays one of Barry's records but he can never pronounce his name properly, he calls him Harry Banilow. Sometimes I think Terry does it on purpose. Then what do I do? Yes, so I get up and have a Sainsbury's bubble bath. Then I get out, cream my knees and elbows. Immac under my arms, put all my make-up on and do my hair. Then of course I have to choose what to wear. Well time's getting on so I go downstairs, he's done all the housework but I have to water the plants. Then I sit and listen to Barry until Maurice comes home. (. . .) He's home at one o'clock. He has tomato soup and two slices of bread and I have a doughnut, a cup of coffee and a five-milligram Librium. No sooner that's done than he goes back to work and I have to have a sleep until he comes back at teatime. Then, while we eat our digestives Maurice tells me all the news; all about the riots and the muggings and the rapes and the old people being murdered (*More emotionally.*) and the blacks kidnapping white women and all the kiddies that's molested by perverts and the animals that's tortured by teenagers and the multiple crashes on the motorways and how people have been trapped inside their cars and been burnt alive.

She continues more normally.

Well, when he's told me all the latest, I have a ten-milligram Librium and he cooks the dinner.

Pause.

Meat, two veg, gravy, tin of fruit and Dream Topping, let's say. Then Gwenda comes round and Maurice and her talk about how the country's going down the drain. Then it's cocoa, two Cadbury's Fingers, Mogadon and bed.

There is a long pause during which time a siren is heard.

Why is John Lennon Wearing a Skirt? *by Claire Dowie*

Why is John Lennon Wearing a Skirt? is a one-woman show about being female. It follows the life and experiences of one woman who doesn't want to be a girl and chooses to pursue her own lifestyle without conforming to stereotypes of 'womanly' behaviour.

In this passage, having fantasised about her ideal experience of the Women's Lib movement she attends her first meeting.

And then I went to a meeting. A women only group. And I said, 'Who's in charge?' and they said, 'We all are.' And they talked about sisterhood and patriarchy and politics – or more to the point, how they hated men. And I said, 'Doesn't anybody hate women? Doesn't anybody hate being a woman? Doesn't anybody hate being thought of as kind and gentle and understanding and supportive and patient and democratic and nurturing and reasonable and non-aggressive and helpful and self-sacrificing and fair-minded and co-operative? Doesn't anybody hate being thought of as nice? Like a biscuit? Doesn't anybody want to be a hero? Doesn't anybody just love what men do and want to do it too? Isn't there anybody here who's insanely jealous that they weren't born a boy? That they weren't born with the opportunity to do anything they wanted to do without having to apologise or justify or explain or feel guilty or awkward or feel like a freak or be ridiculed or persecuted or ostracised or wait till it's fashionable?' And they said, 'No.' And I said, 'What's wrong with me then, why am I such a freak? Why can't I just be a woman, what are you then?' And they said, 'Oppressed.' Fine. Be that then.

Teendreams *by David Edgar and Susan Todd*

Teendreams follows the lives of two women showing how their teenage idealism of the sixties is eroded by the experiences of being a wife, mother and teacher in the seventies.

Rosie, the less politically aware of the two, marries young. As she grows older she comes to resent her husband's repressive attitude towards her need for personal fulfilment. This speech is addressed to a chauvinistic male teacher whom she has just met at a friend's house.

Rosie (*quietly*) When I was nineteen, I was asked to this wedding. And at the reception afterwards, met Howard. We stood near each other, giggled at the speeches, drank the fizzy wine. And then he asked me to go out with him, and I said yes, so out we went, and then he asked, well in a month or so, if I would be engaged to him, and I said yes, and so engaged we were, and then before I knew it I was being asked if I would love and honour and obey, and I said yes, and love and honour and obey I did, and shortly after that I must have stopped the pill, cos I had Damion and three years later I had Sophie, complications and my tubes tied up, and I do not recall, throughout that happy fairy tale, one single, solitary choice at all. I never chose to get engaged. Be married. Have my children. I was chosen. (. . .)

Now, you will know the concept of the Déjà Vu. The feeling, I've done this, been here before. It's quite disturbing. Even more disturbing is the feeling that I had, from time to time, throughout my happy fairy life, a feeling in the night-time, in the darkness, of Non Déjà Vu, a sense of loss of something that I should have been, but hadn't, sense of never really doing, never thinking, anything; a sense of being thought and being done. Which you will doubtless find it hard to understand. Because, although there's limits to your choices, you can choose and map your life. Whereas, my life, and Trisha's and Denise's, aren't like yours, because they are not mappable. They're mapped.

So don't you talk to me, to Frances or to them, about free choice. Cos, on that score, dear Nick, you just don't know you're born.

Cleo, Camping, Emmanuelle and Dick *by* *Terry Johnson*

Cleo, Camping, Emmanuelle and Dick follows the experiences of three major *Carry On* stars during the filming of four different movies at four different periods in time. Over the course of the play the relationship between Sid James, an inveterate womaniser, and Barbara Windsor, an actress married to an East End gangster is revealed to be a true love affair – something that takes both of them by surprise.

Imogen is a fading starlet, first seen in *Carry on Cleo* as a Nubian slave and now playing a bit part in *Camping*. At this point in the play she's just had sex with Sid James in his caravan. She's upper class, pretty and longs to be seen as something more than just a large-breasted bimbo.

Imogen I'm sorry [. . .] I'm always causing arguments. If there's a man and there's me and then someone else there's usually an argument [. . .] I'm surprised you even remembered me. I'm flattered. I mean, who was I then? I was out and about, I know, but I'd barely left LAMDA and honestly I knew nothing. I *was* nothing. This is such a strange business. You get a job, you meet someone, you like them, you maybe sleep with them, the job ends, then you never see them again even though you always say you will. I made some really good friends on *When Dinosaurs Ruled the Earth*, except Raquel of course, but she doesn't make friends she just takes the odd hostage. Thing is I haven't seen anyone since. Except there was a particularly persistent caveman who I did see once but his wife was pregnant and he just cried all evening. Everything's so . . . temporary. That's what's nice about working with you lot; you're one big happy family. I'd love to work with you lot again [. . .] (*She carries on drinking.*) [. . .] You know what I wish? I wish I had smaller breasts. Then I'd get to play some women with small breasts, and they're always the best parts. I'd really like to play women with no breasts at all, you know, like in Ibsen. I should never have done the centrefold. I'm actually very versatile. 'An impressive multifaceted performance'; that's what they said about me as Jenny Grubb in *Loving*. And that wasn't just taking off the glasses and letting my hair down, that was *acting* actually. I was *acting* her repressed sexuality. What I'm saying is, I'm not just some stupid girl from Elmhurst with a fucked knee, you know. I'm not just the Countess of Cleavage; all right? It's so hard to convince people I'm a serious actress, but I really think it's beginning to happen.

My Mother Said I Never Should *by* *Charlotte Keatley*

This play is set in Manchester and looks at the relationship of mother and daughter between four generations of women. Doris is the eldest of these women. This speech takes place at the end of the play, when Doris would have been about twenty-three years old. She has just returned from a picnic where her future husband has proposed to her. She is wearing a 1920s print dress, and is breathless with her hair awry. It is May 1923.

Doris Mother! Mother? Mother! Oh, what do you think! It's happened, happened to me! All the way back on the train I could hardly keep still, I don't know what the other passengers must've thought, but I wouldn't be ladylike. Mother! Come and look. Do I look different? I must look different, I feel as though I've swallowed a firework. Oh it was a lovely, lovely day. We took a picnic, climbed up to the Waterloo memorial, sat in the sunshine and it was after we'd finished the egg and cress; he couldn't wait till after the fruit cake! I felt so – shy, suddenly – I had to just stare and stare at the tablecloth while he was asking, blue and yellow squares, there was an ant struggling to carry a piece of cress across the corner. . . . These are things you remember all your life, I suppose. I didn't think it would be like this.

Pause.

And then we just ran and ran! Talked, made plans. I felt somehow – weedy!

Laughs.

– Sort of silly, for having given in . . . to – love! – Do you know what I mean?

30

Silence.

Mother? We ate your fruit cake on the train, Jack put a paper down so as not to drop crumbs on the velvet upholstery, but then he sat on a strawberry – and oh, I got a grass stain on my frock, but Jack says he'll buy me a new one. *And*, Mother, *and* I got promoted to Head of Infants this morning! Miss Butterworth called me into her office, my heart was in my mouth, I thought she was going to tick me off for this dress being too short! . . . Jack was very proud when I told him, but of course he says I shan't need to work when we're – when we're – oh, of course he's going to ask you first, he's waiting in the front room, I opened the curtains so the neighbours can see – Oh and—

Lights begin to fade.

I've seen just the posy, tiny white flowers, in the window of Ambleton's . . . Oh Mother, I'm so happy. SO HAPPY! I suppose, really and truly, this is the beginning of my life!

*Lights fade to a single spot on **Doris's** face, then snap out.*

A State Affair *by Robin Soans*

Marie is a young drug addict living on an estate in the Buttershaw area of Bradford, 2000.

In A State Affair, a theatre company who had originally worked with Andrea Dunbar, a writer who had lived in and written about the area in the 1980s, returned to find out how, and if, anything had changed in eighteen years. What they discovered was a community now riven by drugs and crime. The writer Robin Soans interviewed people from the estate and placed their words in a dramatic context. All the text, however, is non-fiction.

In this speech Marie describes the circumstances leading up to her first experience of taking heroin.

Marie I've looked in the phone book. There are only two G. Parkers in Shipley. I try the first number and say, 'You don't know me . . . you'll think I'm weird, but I'm trying to find someone.' A voice at the other end said, 'Is that Marie?' It turned out to be Benny, my dad's best friend. He said, 'Your dad's in Greece on holiday 'til next Tuesday.' It turned out my dad was a drug dealer. His house was called The Shop. The next Tuesday we drove to Manchester Airport, but before we go, Benny sat me down and said, 'There's something I have to tell you . . . your dad's in a wheelchair. He broke his neck playing rugby in prison.' At the airport, when Benny sees my dad, he jumps over the barrier, and points to me, and I see my dad's lips form the word 'Marie' . . . and I'm crying by this time. He pushes himself in his wheelchair . . . we're stood in front of each other. He says, 'Oh my daughter, my baby.' All the nights I'd cried at my mum's I'd imagined my dad would be a knight in shining armour . . . and he was. It was party time. It was party time every day there. All this time I hadn't been seeing my mum. Dad got a driver to take us. It was Saturday, so obviously she was at bingo. Six o'clock she turns up pissed. As soon as she saw my dad she said, 'I've had her for the first fucking eighteen years, now it's your turn.' Dad just told the driver to drive. Six weeks later, Benny said, 'Your dad's going out without me, and he's not telling me where . . . my guess is he's got a woman in tow.' The next night I saw my dad go out in a taxi. He was done up to the nines, in one of his fancy waistcoats – he's got about three hundred – two o'clock in the morning he rolls in, and because he's in a wheelchair, all the doors in his house have to slide. He says, 'Have I got a surprise for you?' He gives the sliding door a big push . . . and my mum walks in. She says, 'Hello darling, how are you?' Benny sees my face and takes me into another room. He passes me something on a piece of foil, which I suck up through a tube. I've gone to the toilet, thrown my guts up for half an hour, and then I lie down on my bed, and I'm in heaven. What he gave me was heaven on a piece of foil.

Summer *by Edward Bond*

Summer shows the reunion of two women who were
respectively servant and mistress in an occupied area of
Europe during the war. The mistress collaborated but her
collaboration saved the servant's life. In their meeting the
past is searingly revived.

Marthe was the servant. A gracious woman who is dying
of an incurable disease. She now lives in the old house of
her mistress.

Marthe (*working*)   What's more useless than death? Life without death would be. How could you find anything beautiful if you looked at it forever? You'd grow tired of it. Why fall in love if it lasted forever? When you'd forgiven yourselves a thousand times you'd tire of forgiveness. You'd grow tired of changing the people you loved.

Ann *returns with three folded chairs, opens them and sets them at the table.*

If you ate for eternity why bother to taste what you're eating? You can taste the next meal. When you've cried for one mistake you wouldn't cry for the next. You'd have eternity to put it right. Soon your eyes would be full of sleep. You'd go deaf. You wouldn't listen to voices because they would give you the trouble of answering. Why listen to them? It would be useless to know which was a sparrow or a waterfall. In eternity there would be no future. You'd sit on the ground and turn to stone. Dust would pile up and bury you. If we didn't die we'd live like the dead. Without death there's no life. No beauty, love or happiness. You can't laugh for more than a few hours or weep more than a few days. No one could bear more than our life. Only hell could be eternal. Sometimes life is cruel and death is sudden – that's the price we pay for not being stones. Don't let the lightning strike you or madmen burn your house. Don't give yourself to your enemies or neglect anyone in need. Fight. But in the end death is a friend who brings a gift: life. Not for you but the others. I die so that you might live. Did you call David? Breakfast's ready.

Truly, Madly, Deeply *by Anthony Minghella*

Nina is grieving for her dead lover Jamie. Her grief is so great that Jamie returns as a ghost and Nina finds herself caught between her old life with Jamie and the new life that she was starting to explore without him. She has befriended a special needs teacher, Mark, who is keen to begin a relationship.

At this point the two have met for a date. Nina is distracted and Mark tries to tell her all about himself whilst hopping on one leg. It's now Nina's turn . . .

———————————

Nina Nina Mitchell, I can't believe I'm doing this! Also Capricorn, but also don't believe so I can't make anything of that, think there may be a God, interpreter, I'm starting at the end, I believe in protesting, in the possibility of change, in making this planet more, decent. You know, you see it all the time. I hate what this country is doing to itself, and to the people, and the way we treat other races, visitors, this happens every day . . . well you know, you saw it in the café . . . wrong skin, wrong size, wrong shape: you're lost . . . or wrong religion, wrong ideology, wrong class, it makes me so! Oh, do you want me to be more personal? Um, okay, parents alive, Gloucestershire, teachers, him Geography, her History, so holidays it would be *Dad, where are we? Mum, have we been here before?* I like them, I have a sister, Claire, I love her, she has a family and a husband I can't stand who keeps climbing everything – climbs socially, in business, and now – finally – has started climbing mountains. Um, they have a son, Harry. She's pregnant again for the second time, their son is my nephew, and I adore him. Did I say I was born in Stratford? Well, I was and do you know that I pay to do this once a week, to talk, that's where I was going the other day when I saw you on the bus, to my woman, the Burge, Doctor Burge. The only difference is there you get fifty minutes and no exercise and here it seems to spill out, and I play the piano, I love Bach, I have rats, I'm in a mess, I live alone, I haven't always, not always—

The Art of Success *by Nick Dear*

The Art of Success is set in Hogarth's London where corruption, dissolution and disease are rife. Hogarth struggles to establish a copyright on his engravings but with little thought as to whether his subjects wish to have their image sold to the public.

Louisa is Hogarth's prostitute lover called upon to perform those services which he would never ask of his wife.

———————————

Louisa (*shivers*) Wind off the Thames blows down the avenues, round the rotunda, through the triumphal arches and directly up my skirt. I must have the coldest legs in England. A sailor in a Bermondsey cellar said that in China they tell of a wind disease, a cold, cold wind blowing round the body, typhoon in your arms and legs, whispering draughts at the back of your skull. I told him I think I've got it, mate, it all sounds dead familiar. He laughed and bit my nipple with splintering teeth. What I would have loved, at that moment, what I longed for, was that all the air would whoosh out of me like a burst balloon, and I sink down to nothing at his feet, and teach the disbelieving rat a lesson. Here I am out in all weathers, all the entrances and exits in my body open to the elements day and freezing night, what's to stop the gale when it comes in and fills me? And blows round my bones for ever? – Wait, is he walking this way? That dragoon? He looks so sad . . . doesn't he look sad . . . I don't know, they call this place a pleasure garden, I've never seen such misery, I'd christen it the garden of wind and disappointment, or cold and frosted cunt.

Jane *has entered, unseen. She listens.*

Is he coming over here? Come along, then, miss, get all your gusts and breezes together . . . Nice time with an old windbag, soldier? It's not wearing any knickers.

Oleanna *by David Mamet*

Carol, a college student, comes to her professor John to discuss her grades. Carol is nervous and unsure of herself and John, whilst attempting to listen to her problems, is distracted by his need to meet with his wife to buy a new house. Carol joins a 'group' who empower her with the language of political correctness. She brings a complaint against John to the faculty of the college, resulting in his failure to achieve a tenured post at the college and his suspension. This then means that he loses the house he was hoping to buy. In effect, Carol has ruined John's life both personally and professionally.

At this point in the play John, having lost his job, has invited Carol, reluctantly, to his office to apologise to her. Carol explains to him the feelings of all his female students, as personified in the 'Group'.

Carol For Christ's sake. Who the *hell* do you think that you are? You want a post. You want unlimited power. To do and to say what you want. As it pleases you – Testing, Questioning, Flirting [. . .] Excuse me, one moment, will you?

(*She reads from her notes.*)

The twelfth: 'Have a good day, dear.'

The fifteenth: 'Now, don't *you* look fetching . . .'

April seventeenth: 'If you girls would come over here . . .' I saw you. I saw you, Professor. For two semesters sit there, stand there and exploit our, as you thought, 'paternal prerogative,' and what is that but rape: I swear to God. You asked me in here to explain something to me, as a child, that I did not understand. But I came to explain something to you. You Are Not God. You ask me why I came? I came here to instruct you.

(She produces his book.)

And your book? You think you're going to show me some 'light'?
You *'maverick.'* Outside of tradition. No, no, *(She reads from the
book's liner notes.) 'of* that fine tradition of *inquiry.* Of Polite
skepticism' . . . and you say you believe in free intellectual discourse.
YOU BELIEVE IN NOTHING. YOU BELIEVE IN NOTHING AT ALL.
[. . .] why do you question, for one moment, the committee's
decision refusing your tenure? Why do you question your
suspension? You believe in what *you call* freedom of thought. Then,
fine. *You* believe in freedom-of-thought *and* a home, and, *and*
prerogatives for your kid, *and* tenure. And I'm going to tell you. You
believe *not* in 'freedom of thought,' but in an elitist, in, in a
protected hierarchy which rewards you. And for whom you are the
clown. And you mock and exploit the system which pays your rent.
You're wrong. I'm not wrong. You're wrong. You think that I'm full
of hatred. I know what you think I am. [. . .] You think I am a
frightened, repressed, confused, I don't know, abandoned young
thing of some doubtful sexuality, who wants, power and revenge.
(Pause) Don't you? *(Pause)* [. . .] Isn't that better? And I feel that that
is the first moment which you've treated me with respect. For you
told me the truth. *(Pause)* I did not come here, as you are assured, to
gloat. Why would I want to gloat? I've profited nothing from your,
your, as you say, your 'misfortune.' I came here, as you did me the
honor to *ask* me here, I came here to *tell* you something.

(Pause) That I think . . . that I think you've been wrong. That I think
you've been terribly wrong. Do you hate me now? *(Pause)*

Up To You, Porky *by Victoria Wood*

Up To You, Porky is a compilation of comedy sketches and monologues. This speech has no specific context and is entirely open to interpretation by the actor.

————————————

Guide Right, I'm your official guide. Now before I show you round, I'll just fill you in on a few details, as we call them. As you can see, we're standing in the hall of the Haworth Parsonage, where Haworth's parson, the Reverend Brontë, lived here with his daughters, the famous Brontë sisters, now, alas, no longer with us – but they have left us their novels, which I've not read, being more of a Dick Francis nut. Now, if you pass by me into the parlour (mind my vaccination) . . . This is what was known in those days as a parlour, somewhat similar to our lounge-type sitting-room affair in modern technology. I'm afraid the wallpaper isn't the original period to which we're referring to, it is actually Laura Ashley, but I think it does give some idea of what life must have been like in a blustery old Yorkshire community of long ago.

That portrait on the wall is actually of Charlotte Brontë, one of the famous Brontë sisters, and of course to us she may seem a rather gloomy-looking individual; but you must remember these days she'd have a perm or blusher, or I suppose even drugs would have helped her maintain a more cheerful attitude. In fact, she'd probably not be dead if she was alive today. Now if you'd like to hutch through to the Reverend Brontë's study. . . . This is a typical study in which to do studying – as you can see there's a table, chair . . . (oh my poncho, I've been looking for that . . .) and I like to imagine this elderly old gentleman hunched over a sermon, probably thinking, 'Where's my cocoa, I suppose those darn girls are in the middle of another chapter,' or something like that he may have been thinking – we just can't be sure . . . Of course he died eventually, unfortunately. You must remember this is an extremely exposed part of the United Kingdom, I mean, it's May now, and I'm still having to slip that polo-neck under my bolero.

Beached *by Kevin Hood*

Maria, a streetwise girl in her late teens has run away with
Pete, an ex-schoolfriend. Pete has attacked Maria's father
during a bungled burglary attempt and may well have
accidentally murdered him. The teenagers are both spending the night on the beach in a bird sanctuary. For both of
them this is proving to be a night of bleakness as they both
face the realisation that the reality of their lives is not as
rosy as their daydreams.

At this point Maria has decided to leave Pete. Pete starts
to panic about the possible murder of her father, Giovanni.
Maria decides to tell Pete about her past relationship with
her father.

———————————

Maria (*pause. She faces* **Pete**) I'll tell you a story, shall I? 'Bout when I was younger. Thirteen. And 'im, on 'is own with me. Me growin' up, 'im wonderin' 'ow I'm goin' to turn out. Well . . . every time 'e goes down the pub, 'e locks me in. With me chocolate and me crisps and the portable telly. And at first I can't work it out: And then it dawns. (*Pause.*) What 'e thinks is, first fella I see – I'm on me back with me legs wide open, waitin' for it. That's what 'e thinks. [. . .] I don't like that. I ain't 'avin' that. So . . . one night, one Monday night I'm out the winder and leggin' it down Lewisham with some of the naughty girls from school. Disco. (*Pause.*) I mean, what did I expect, eh? Moonlight in me Chianti? Candlelight on me chips? Well, what I got was warm lager, lots and lots of warm lager, and these three fellas, this band, in the back of their van . . . one after the other.

Silence.

Didn't know what was 'appenin'. Thirteen and pissed, see. (*Pause.*) Long walk 'ome, I tell ya. (*Pause.*) But . . . by the time 'e's openin' the front door there I am, tucked up in bed, all safe and sound. With this 'andful of J-Cloths and ice between my legs. And prayin', oh sweet Maria, prayin' I can 'old off cryin' long enough, 'cause every particle tells me if 'e finds out, 'e's goin' to kill me, I mean really kill me. But it's *all right*. Door opens. 'Buona notte, Mariucca'. Papa . . . and I almost cry, I almost . . . the thing that saves me is the smell on 'im, beer. That smell. Them fellas. 'Im. (*Pause.*) That was the last of 'im for me. No, Peter, I ain't worried about Giovanni.

Our Country's Good *by Timberlake Wertenbaker*

Our Country's Good takes as its basis the performance of Farquhar's *The Recruiting Officer* by a cast of convicts in Australia in 1789.

Liz, angry and unpenitent convict, is playing the part of Melinda. She is suspected of having taken part in a raid on the stores and has been sentenced to be hanged. In this speech she talks for the first time about her past and why she is in a penal colony. Like her fellow convicts she is in chains.

Liz Luck? Don't know the word. Shifts its bob when I comes near. Born under a ha'penny planet I was. Dad: he was a nibbler, don't want to get crapped. Mum leaves, wants the water of life. Five brothers, I'm the only titter. I takes in washing. Then. My own father. Lady's walking down the street, takes her wiper. She screams, he's shoulder-clapped, says, it's not me, Sir, it's Lizzie, look, she took it. I'm stripped, beaten in the street, everyone watching. That night, I take my dad's cudgel and try to kill him, I prig all his clothes and go to my older brother. He don't want me, another tooth. Liz, he says, why trine for a make, when you can wap for a winne. I'm no dimber mort, I says. Don't ask you to be a swell mollisher, Sister, coves want Miss Laycock, don't look at your mug. So I begin to sell my mother of saints. I thinks I'm in luck when I meet the swell cove. He's a bobcull. He says to me, it's not enough to sell your mossie face, Lizzie, it don't bring no shiners no more. Shows me how to spice the swells. So. Swell has me up the wall, flashes a rum thimble, I lifts it. But one time I stir my stumps too slow, the swell squeaks beef, the snoozie hears, I'm nibbed. It's up the ladder to rest, I thinks when I goes up before the fortune teller, but no, the judge's a bobcull, I nap the King's pardon and it's seven years across the herring pond. Jesus Christ the hunger on the ship, sea crabs won't touch me no rantum scantum, no food, but here, the Governor says, new life, you could nob it here, Lizzie, I think, bobcull gov, this niffynaffy play, not too much work, good crew of rufflers, Kable, Arscott, but no, Ross don't like my mug, I'm nibbed again and now it's up the ladder to rest for good. Well. Lizzie Morden's life. And you, Wisehammer, how did you get here?

The Pitchfork Disney *by Philip Ridley*

Hayley shares a home with her 'twin' brother, Presley. Both of them are reclusive. Following the supposed death of their parents the siblings have stayed at home, only venturing out at night and living on chocolate bars. They bicker and squabble, telling each other stories about their childhood, reminiscing about their early relationship with their parents.

In the following speech Hayley explains to Presley why she doesn't like to go shopping.

Hayley And I told you what happened. How when I got to the end of the street a pack of dogs appeared. One started to chase me. I was running. Running and screaming. The other dogs chased me as well. All of them howling and snarling like wolves. They chased me over the wasteground. [. . .] Through the old car park and into the derelict church. And still the dogs chased me. There I was, standing at the altar, with seven rabid animals coming down the aisles towards me. I picked up some old bibles and threw them. Did no good. The dogs ripped the bibles to pieces. I was so afraid. [. . .] Then one of the dogs made a lunge for me. I jumped up. Reached above me. Caught hold of something. It was smooth. Cool. Solid. I started to climb. Like climbing a tree. And I was halfway up before I realised I was climbing the marble crucifix and my chest was pressed close to the chest of Christ. It felt so comforting and safe. Then a dog bit at my feet. Pulled my shoe off. My toes were bleeding. A drop of blood landed in the open mouth of the dog. It went berserk. Started to climb the crucifix. I scarpered higher, wrapped my legs round the waist of our Saviour, clung onto the crown of thorns for all I was worth. Then the base of the crucifix started to crumble. It rocked from side to side. Any minute it might fall and send me into the pack of dogs. Like a Christian to the hungry lions. I was so scared. So I kissed the lips of Christ. I said, 'Save me. Don't let the cruifix fall'. But the crucifix fell just the same. I crashed to the floor. The dogs nibbled at my bloodied fingers. I'm going to be eaten alive, I thought. Eaten by savage dogs. I screamed, 'Help me! Help me!'. And then . . . gun shots! I flinch at every one. I look round. The seven dogs are dead. Blood oozing from holes in their skulls. I feel sick. A Priest approaches me. He is holding a rifle. He asks me if I'm all right. I tell him I am. He says, 'Did you come for confession?'. And I say, 'Yes'. Because I think that's what he wants to hear and I owe him something for saving my life. So I go into confession with him and he asks me what I've done wrong. I tell him I can't think of anything. He says, 'Don't be stupid. No one's perfect'. I know he's right. I know there's something I've done. Something that made me a naughty girl once. But I can't think of what it is. I tell him I can't think of anything. He tells me to think harder. I can feel him getting angry and frustrated. He wants to forgive me but I'm not giving him the chance. Finally, I say, 'I kissed the lips of Christ and they tasted of chocolate'. He calls me a sinner and says I must repent. I ask him if I can be forgiven and he says, 'No! Your sins are too big'. I'm crying when I leave the church. I vow never to go shopping again.

The Great Celestial Cow *by Sue Townsend*

The Great Celestial Cow is about the lives of Asian women in England and the difficulties they have to face through racial prejudice and cultural difference. Bibi is a westernized girl of eighteen. She finds it hard to reconcile her education with the submissive role she is expected to take as a daughter and prospective wife. In this speech Bibi is talking directly to the audience, having sneaked out for a night's dancing. It is set in the loo in the Palais, at midnight.

Bibi Well, I had a brilliant time tonight. Debauchery galore there was. I've been with every bloke in the Palais – must be 200. I came in at eight and it's Cinderella time now. So it's not bad going is it? It's my legs you see. One glimpse and the English blokes are sitting on their haunches panting for it and I'm so depraved and corrupted by the West that I let them have it. You see I've no morality of my own. No respect for my body. I've got three 'A' levels but no intelligence. I can't be trusted, after all I'm only twenty. Mum knows I come here. There's nothing I wouldn't tell her – well the odd thing. But Mum doesn't count for much in our family. When it's not at Sketchleys I keep me gear in a black plastic bag in Mum's wardrobe, next to her bucket. It's pathetic. Here I am an Asian girl caught in a culture clash. See these things each side of my head? Inverted commas. Now the English *are* lucky – they don't have family problems.

No, they sit around in shafts of sunlight eating cornflakes, then get up and run around meadows in slow motion. One in four that is. The other three are undergoing divorce or family therapy. Yes we all jostle for space on the *Guardian* Women's Page. There's me, cheek by jowl with 'Shall I, a committed Socialist, send my Rupert to public school?' Now that *would* make you toss and turn at night. I'm educated. I'm healthy, and I'll make myself some sort of life. But until then I'll change in the bog. Me mum's got enough on her plate.

Pause.

If anyone asks, I've been babysitting.

Silly Cow *by Ben Elton*

Doris is the hugely successful writer of a supremely bitchy and unpleasant column for a tabloid newspaper. An actress whose performance she ripped to shreds in one of her articles is suing her for defamation of character. On the morning of the trial she meets with the editor of a rival tabloid to sign a deal, committing to writing for a European rival.

In the following speech she explains to Sid, the editor, her history and how she has paid her dues to reach this level of fame and notoriety.

———————

Doris You're not the only one who'll be giving things up, Sidney Skinner! You're not the only one who's had to work hard for everything they've got! While you were sneaking around Hollywood trying to buy photos of Jackie Onassis with her fun bags flying, I was dogsbody on the *Preston Clarion*, and I mean dogsbody. [. . .] Yes, and I'm never going back. These last few years I've finally got a grip of *la dolce vita* and I'm sticking my talons in deep. I am never again going to get up at five thirty on a rainy morning to report on a sheep-dog trial, I am never again going to cover the Liberal candidate in a by-election, and I am never again going to review another show at Preston Rep [. . .] There was this appalling old ham; I'd watched him every three weeks for two and a half years, and whatever part he played, he did his Noël Coward impression. Hamlet's ghost, Noël Coward. *The Crucible*, Noël Coward; *Mother Courage*, Noël Coward. Imagine what the old fart was like when he actually had to play in a Noël Coward – his accent got so clipped I swear he was only using the first letter of each word. So please believe me, Sidney, I am never going back to that.

Adult Child/Dead Child *by Claire Dowie*

Adult Child/Dead Child follows the life of a disturbed and
abused child as it grows up and attempts to come to terms
with the world. It is a one-person show.

_____

My father was an actor
professional pretender
pretended to be a father

pretended to have feelings
pretended enthusiasm
demanded perfection
demanded perfection
100% do it right, do it the best
be brainy, be sporty, be talented, be good
academic athlete
well mannered, polite, know it all, do it all
100% do it right, do it the best
I cried, I would cry
I would cry & I failed
always failed
for my professional pretending father
& his daughter, the apple of his eye
who could do no wrong.

I remember being in the garden of our old house. I was about six or seven & there were friends of my parents visiting. I can't remember now who, but somebody gave me a cowboy & indian set. This was a cowboy hat & gun & holster & a tin star with the word 'sheriff' on it & an indian feather thing with a band on it for a hat & a tomahawk & my dad said let's play with it & first he was the cowboy & I was the indian & everybody was watching & I ran at him with my tomahawk but he shot me so I lost & then we changed round & I was the cowboy & my dad was the indian but before I could shoot him he threw the tomahawk & it hit my head & he said it was Custer's last stand & everybody laughed (I thought he said 'custard' & I didn't understand) & he said I was hopeless because I died twice & I didn't want to play with my cowboy & indian set anymore but later on that night I decided to be the indian & sneak up on him quietly but when I sneaked into their bedroom & jumped on him with my tomahawk he woke up. Didn't act like a cowboy, acted like an angry father.

Down the Line *by Paul Mercier*

Deirdre is the youngest of four in a suburban Dublin family. Politicised by university she's leaving home for the first time. Her boyfriend, Conor, helps her to move out. Deirdre loves her parents but despises their middle-class, suburban attitudes.

In the following speech Deirdre explains to Conor her feelings of betrayal the first time they visited the 'family farm' only to discover that the mother's connections to it were tenuous.

Deirdre (*checking garage and locking it*) We were driving back to Dublin one time and she asked the dad to go on a detour. And Dad said he wanted to get home. But no, she was going to drop by and say hello. And we cheered in the car. We were going to Mammy's farm. And on that farm there were some cows, ee eye ee eye yo. [. . .] The moo moos were there all right. But everyone else had vanished. They must have heard she was coming and ran into the fields. Jesus, that Angelus vibe. Sunday. Dead heat like this. Dad said he was staying in the car. And the four of us raced up this long avenue of tall jaded sycamore trees. Mam was shouting at us not to disgrace ourselves. And this dog showed up barking like hell and snapping at Liam's heels.

But the place was locked up. We looked everywhere for a key so we could get in and she told us there was no key. And then she lost her temper with the dog. And then Liam started bawling because he fell into a lump of cowshit and the flies were swarming all around him. And there was mammy walking around the outside of the cottage as if she were on a pilgrimage, locked out of her own home. Liam blubbering and pulling at her skirt with his shitty hands.

I saw her looking hard through the small window of the house. Her two hands over her squinting eyes as if she were trying to see the time on the clock. We all took a window and did the same thing. We asked her what she was looking for. She said – 'Let's go home now.' And as she dragged us back down the avenue, she stopped, looked back and muttered under her breath that she never liked the kip anyway. And this breeze came up and the leaves of the sycamores rustled like a million whispering voices. She nearly ran, hurried us out the gate and bundled us into the car. Dad said nothing. He had the engine running all the time. He just put the foot down and we were gone.

Bazaar & Rummage *by Sue Townsend*

Bazaar And Rummage is a comedy set in a church hall
where a jumble sale is being held by a trainee social worker,
three agoraphobics and Gwenda, an ex-agoraphobic and
volunteer social worker.

Gwenda acts as a lifeline for the three women. As the
women become more confident being out in the world,
Gwenda starts to feel threatened by their independence and
becomes increasingly emotional. Here Gwenda is talking to
the trainee social worker, Fliss, whilst unpacking boxes of
jumble.

———————————

Gwenda (*unaware that* **Fliss** *has gone, she continues stacking the books into paperback and hardback piles*) I read a lot when I was a girl. Asthmatics are usually well read, you have noticed? I had Enid Blyton's complete works. Complete. My father brought one home every Friday night without fail. My mother had a quarter pound of Mint Imperials, father had two ounces of Shag and I had my new Enid Blyton. I'm sure that's why I'm quite without racial prejudice you know. Golly, Wog and Nigger were always my favourites, they were naughty to the other toys, but they always took their punishment well.

She finds **Black Beauty**.

Black Beauty! I could go on *Mastermind* with *Black Beauty* as my main subject.

Quickly.

What was Black Beauty's mother's name?

Carefully.

Duchess.

Quickly.

Who was the first man to break Black Beauty in?

Carefully.

Squire Gordon.

Quickly.

What lesson did Squire Gordon teach Black Beauty?

Softly.

You must never start at what you see, nor bite nor kick, nor have any will of your own. But always do your master's will, even though you may be very tired or hungry. That was more or less what father taught me. It's kept me in good stead, service first self second.

An Experienced Woman Gives Advice *by* *Iain Heggie*

The setting is a Sunday morning in the garden of a Scottish tenement building, divided into flats. Nancy has just had a one-night stand with Kenny. She meets Bella, an older woman in the garden and begins telling her all about her evening. She's unaware that Bella is actually Kenny's lover.

Nancy Good! Well. I was out with my pals, so I was. Sitting round a table. A wee social drink. When *he* comes up. (Kenny!) *Picks me out.* Asks me to dance. Me. That was *so* brave. I could have said 'no'. I could have played hard to get. But there was just *no* resisting him. So that was it. Well, it wasn't quite it. You won't catch me giving myself away for a drink and a bag of nuts. Oh no. So. I sat him down and got him to tell me all about himself. The life story! For a boy his age. Lives with an older woman apparently. She was his teacher. The course is nearly over. He's got chance of work elsewhere. London possibly. I told him: 'You can't let this older woman hold you back. You've got your future to think about. You're not doing her any favours. She's got a lonely life on the shelf to get used to. The longer you let her cling on the harder it will be for her in the long run.' So with experience like that he's had. How could I resist? So of course, I gave him permission to invite me back to his place. And he did. So. Back we come. Up the stairs. In. Gorgeous place. Decorated. Carpeted. Centrally heated. Into the living-room. Sits me down. Drinks. Music playing. Dim lighting state. (Awful, awful glamorous.) The doorbell. Kenny goes. And he walks in with this *not at all bad-looking* guy. A guy called Irving. Irving! Who has no sooner sat down till he starts *making eyes*. At *me*. So, of course, Kenny marches him out to bed. Next thing Kenny back in saying: 'Sorry about that.' I say: 'Who's Irving?' Kenny says: 'How should I know?' That kind of night. Thrill a minute, you know. (*She laughs.*)   ·

Waking Up *by Dario Fo and Franca Rame*

A young female factory worker oversleeps and frantically tries to prepare herself and her baby for the forthcoming day – just as she is ready to leave she realizes she has lost her housekeys. In an attempt to retrace her steps she re-enacts the events of the previous evening. At this point she has just reached the stage of reliving the row she had with her husband. The play is a one-woman show.

She mimes turning on him in a rage.

Wife 'Listen, Stupid,' I tell him, 'I don't need to listen to feminists or radicals or anybody else to find out what a shitty life we lead. We both work like dogs and we never have a minute to talk. We never talk to each other! Is that marriage? Like does it ever even enter your mind to think about what's going on inside me? How I feel? Ever ask me if I'm tired . . . if you could give me a hand? Ha!'

Mimes bearing down on him threateningly.

'Who does the cooking? Me! Who does the washing up? Me! Who does the shopping? Me! And who does the death-defying financial acrobatics so we can get through to the end of the month? Me me me! And I'm working full time at the factory, remember. Your dirty socks . . . who washes them eh? How many times have you washed my socks? We should talk to each other, Luigi! We never talk. I mean it's okay with me that your problems are my problems but why can't my problems be your problems too instead of yours being ours and mine being only mine. I just want us to live together . . . not just in the same place. We should talk to each other! But what do we do? You come home from work, watch the telly and go to bed. Day after day it's always the same. Oh, except for Sundays.'

Scornfully.

'Hooray hooray it's football day! Every Sunday off you go to watch twenty-two idiots in their underpants kicking a ball around and some other mentally deficient maniac dashing up and down blowing a whistle!' He . . . that Luigi . . . he went purple in the face! You'd think I'd insulted his mother. 'How could a person like *you* ever know the first thing about sport?'

Brief pause.

Not the best thing he could've said, really.

With relish.

I freaked. 'Who the fuck would want to?' I shouted at him. And then I really started raving on like a lunatic. Oh I said it all. Everything! I screamed at him, he yelled back at me, I screamed louder, he yelled louder . . . we were just about shouting the building down. So finally I said 'Right! If this is marriage we've made a mistake!' And I picked up my mistake and I walked out.

The Age of Consent *by Peter Morris*

Stephanie is the ambitious, show-business mum of a small girl, Raquel. Stephanie sees Raquel as her ticket out of poverty and is determined for her child to be a show business star. Having trained her child that the three 'Ts' of entertainment are 'Talent, Teeth and Tits' Stephanie explains how she and Raquel started in the entertainment industry. It is clear that Stephanie is considerably more interested in herself than in the welfare of her child.

————————————

Stephanie I mean, I was nineteen when I had her. She's six now. And that's been, what? Six years on my own. I've no family to speak of, to lend a hand in raising her, and as for being a *single* mummy, the gentleman in question seemed to think of his role largely in terms of anonymous sperm donation, conducted under slightly less hygienic conditions than usual. I like to say to Raquel, with me and your Darth – that's what I call had daddy now, I call him Darth, like the faceless dark lord of evil in *Star Wars* – I say, with me and your Darth it was panda bear sex, because a panda bear *eats shoots and leaves*. Get it? God forbid that Darth should *ever* send his daughter a brass farthing in child support, or a gift certificate for Top Shop, or a couple of Max Factor Misty Pink Lip Glosses, anything that a girl of Raquel's age might possibly appreciate. The silence from that man is deafening and, to be fair, I'm not really sure where he is now, since initially I met him on holiday at Kusadasi and the address I had for him in this country may now be out of date. [. . .] But what it comes down to is money, right. And that's when I started thinking, well, I think Raquel and I were watching Crufts on the telly and I thought to myself, right, child-rearing, such as it is, you've just got to be firm and communicate in one-syllable commands, and then the rest of it's down to breeding and grooming. I mean, not that Raquel is dog-like in any way, but let's fact it. Child Stars, yeah? The only difference between a prize poodle and a Bonnie Langford is the length of the ringlets. With some discipline I could put Raquel's natural maturity and outgoingness to a good use. I mean, I want Raquel to be the best she can be. This could give her focus. [. . .] But you have no idea how energised I am. I am completely happy and spending my days teaching Raquel to sing, to dance, and even some elocution and fencing on the side. I finally feel like a mother.

Joyriders *by Christina Reid*

Joyriders is set in Belfast where a group of young offenders are taking part in a government Youth Opportunities Programme scheme. The aim of the scheme is to provide them with 'helpful' skills, enabling them to find employment at the end of the year. The young people, however, are less optimistic about their futures.

Sandra is a cynical, abrasive seventeen-year-old. She copes with her situation by maintaining her defences and rarely, if ever, revealing her true feelings. In this speech she has just been proposed to by Arthur, a fellow YOP schemer.

Sandra The one an' only time I ever wore a white lace frock, Arthur, was for my first communion . . . an' my mother parades me down the road to get my photo tuk, an' she says to the photographer, 'Isn't our Sandra a picture? Won't she make a beautiful bride?' an' I told her I was never gonna get married, an' she got all dewy-eyed because she thought I wanted to be a nun. . . . A bride of Christ, or forty years' hard labour . . . my mother thinks anything in between is a mortal sin. . . . She married a big child like you, Arthur, an' what did it get her . . . eight kids an' twenty years' cookin' cleanin' an' survivin' on grants an' handouts. . . . You're too like my da fer comfort. Fulla big plans that'll come to nuthin' because yer too soft an' yer too easy-goin' an' havin' all that money won't make ye any different. Whatever you da an' the rest of your ones don't steal from ye, the world will. They'll ate ye alive. . . . You know what the big trick in this life is? It's knowin' what ye don't want, an' I don't want to be a back-seat joyrider, content to sit and giggle behind the fellas who do the stealin' an' the drivin' . . . I stole a car once . . . all by myself . . . I never told nobody, doin' it was enough . . . I just drove it roun' them posh streets in South Belfast until it ran outa petrol, an' then I walked home. Didn't need to boast about it the way the fellas do . . . just doin' it was enough. . . . When the careers' officer come to our school, he asked me what I wanted to do, an' I says, 'I wanna drive roun' in a big car like yer woman outa Bonnie and Clyde, an' rob banks,' an' he thought I was takin' a hand out him, so I says, 'All right then, I'll settle fer bein' a racin' driver.' An' he says, 'I'd advise you to settle for something less fantastic, Sandra.' . . . They're all the same. They ask ye what ye wanta be, an' then they tell ye what yer allowed to be. . . . Me wantin' to be a racin' driver is no more fantastical than Maureen believin' the fairy stories . . . dilly day-dream, just like her mother before her . . . somewhere over the rainbow, bluebirds die . . .

Spoonface Steinberg *by Lee Hall*

Spoonface Steinberg is a seven-year-old Jewish child. She's profoundly autistic and is dying of cancer. A monologue play, *Spoonface Steinberg* explores the meaning of faith, illness and love.

Spoonface is never self-pitying. At this point in the play she explains why she is unafraid of death.

———————————

Spoonface Concentration camps were these places where they took Jewish people to burn – this is what the doctor said – he said that there were loads of people and they all had to sleep on one bunk and that – and the Nazis shot them and then they starved them and it was horrible for his poor Mam because she was just little – in the whole history of the world there has never been anything as awful as the concentration camps, but what happened to the poor people there was to show that they never gave up hope – and that never mind the worse thing that could happen to people they could not stop them from being human beings [. . .] And the doctor said that his Grandma used to be a singer of the opera before she went to this place – and in them days everyone loved the opera – not like now when everyone likes Take That [*Or relevant boy/girl band of the moment.*] – and when they would put the lights out – all the poor women on the bunks would think of their husbands who were never to be seen – and they would ask Grandma Bernstein to sing – and in the sad dark she would sing – sing to all the poor skinny women – and she sang all the songs what she knew in the opera – and she sang for the poor people in the bunks – and all the poor people who had died – and she sang for the children of the people to come – and that was very important to everyone to have such songs to be sung – and then I would play the music and in the heart of it I could hear the singing of the poor Grandma on her bunk – and the poor children who wrote their pictures on the wall – and even in the darkest place there was someone with such a beautiful song to sing.

Made in Bangkok *by Anthony Minghella*

A group of five travellers come to Bangkok for a mixed trip of business and pleasure – for most of them the pleasure is of a sexual and exploitative nature. Frances, the only woman of the party, is unhappily married to Stephen. She is an intelligent, gentle woman gradually becoming more aware of her unhappiness both in her work and her marriage. In this scene she is talking to her lover, the only other member of the group to whom she can communicate.

Frances No, not because of Stephen. I used to listen to this couple above me, at night – I'm talking about in London, years ago – and they used to have sex all the time. Great long loud sessions, really long and really loud and I used to lie in the dark and strain to listen, to hear them, screw up my eyes to catch the whole performance and imagine it: and my face used to go so hot . . . I remember that sensation: the sense of my face going hot, and straining to hear and these great groans and gasps and cries. You'd see them in the day time – this girl was perfectly ordinary, honestly, you wouldn't have given her a second look . . . a quiet hello, she'd be gone, and I'd know she has these fantastic orgasms. And I remember waking up one night and – being woken by this familiar noise – and straining to hear and my face going hot and then realizing it wasn't them, it was a baby, it was a baby half crying and it was Christopher, my son, and we weren't even in the same flat any more by this time and I'd woken, hardly woken, and made myself come to the sound of my son crying, waiting for me to feed him. I've been staring at the pool and it's black and I've been trying to remember that room, what it looked like: the room underneath the couple. And I can't. Where does it belong, our fantasy world? Do you know?

The Lament for Arthur Cleary *by Dermot Bolger*

Kathy is the eighteen-year-old girlfriend of Arthur, an older man. The two meet at a dance and are attracted to each other but both shy away from the relationship because of their age difference. The play is set in Ireland although it is also set in a limbo land as Arthur comes to realise that he is actually dead.

At this point in the play Kathy explains to a friend about the last time she saw Arthur . . .

Kathy He was waiting for me along the quays, staring at the water as usual. I didn't think I'd have the courage. Arthur, I'm sorry,' I said . . . 'it's just too big an age gap, it's not right.' He never spoke, Sharon, his face looked old, suddenly, like all the air had drained from it. [. . .] All the way home, felt like throwing myself from the bus. I came in, Sharon, saw my father, just sitting, staring at the television. And I remembered a man who feared no other, a brown wage packet left on an oilskin table. If he could only cry, I could stay with him, but his kind were never taught how to show grief. I need to learn to breathe. Sharon, I need Arthur and I don't know how to ask him, to teach me . . . to wake up and not be afraid of what the day will bring. (*Pause.*) I've packed a bag, Sharon. If he'll take me in I'll go to him, or I'll go somewhere else, anywhere, but I don't fit here any more. (*Pause.*) Will you be glad for me?

City Sugar *by Stephen Poliakoff*

Nicola is a shy and inarticulate sixteen-year-old girl living in Leicester. She has potentially a great deal of violence within her. She enters a local radio contest run by Leonard Brazil, the disc jockey. He becomes fascinated by Nicola and contrives for her to win through to the final heat of the competition. In this speech she has been asked by the radio presenter to describe her feelings while at a pop concert.

Nicola Oh . . . and . . .

Lost for words, she is extremely nervous.

—and then we went inside . . . and the concert . . . and it was them of course, and it was, you know . . . well it was all squashed – and some people rushed up and fought to get close – and there was a bit of biting, and that sort of thing, when they called out to us; they seemed a long way off – a very long way away, in their yellow and everything. They weren't loud – but they made you feel – I felt something come up, you know, a little sort of . . .

A second of slight clenched feeling.

I got, you know, a bit worked up inside . . . they were moving very slowly on stage like they'd been slowed down, made me feel strange – then they held things up, waved it at us, smiling and everything, they waved yellow scarves, Ross had a bit of yellow string he waved, I think it was, a bit of yellow rope, and I half wanted to kick the girl in front of me or something because I couldn't see; all the way through I had to look at her great back, pressed right up against it. I remember I half wanted to *get at it*. Move it. And I nearly dropped a ring.

She pulls at her finger.

I'd been pulling at, put it on specially.

Very nervous, she smiles.

If you drop anything it's gone for ever you know – can't bend down if you're standing—

Smiles.

and if you drop yourself . . . then you'd be gone. When you rush out at the end, you can see all the millions of things that have been dropped shining all over the floor, nobody gets a chance to pick them up. And then it was finished – you know, the concert, and I came outside. It was cold, I was feeling a bit funny. Just walked along out there and I thought maybe I was bleeding. I looked but I wasn't. Some people like to be after a concert . . . but I wasn't.

Can't Stand Up for Falling Down *by*
Richard Cameron

The play follows the relationship between three women all
of whom are interconnected by their relationship with the
same violent man. Lynette has married this man, Royce,
and is now a victim of domestic violence. In this speech she
describes one of their violent arguments.

———————————

Lynette Royce has now moved into the back bedroom, thank God. It's been a bit of a time, these last few weeks. I got a knife on the bedroom door lock and managed to get the paint off so it works, I can lock it at night now. Makes it a bit safer. I just don't know what he might do next, after the things he's said to me. Coming in, throwing things. Spoiling things in the house. What's the point of trying to keep things nice? I keep my room clean, I make my own meals when he's out. It's like a pigsty down there.

I tried to clean it up after he'd pulled everything out of the kitchen cupboard and smashed it, but I cut my hand quite bad on a bit of glass from the sauce bottle, I think it was, and I had to leave it. I should have had stitches really. It's funny, I thought it was tomato ketchup.

'Serves you fucking right,' he says. 'Cleaning up. You're always cleaning up. Leave it. Fucking LEAVE IT!' and something's exploded in my head and he must have hit my ear. My hand's full of blood but it's my ear that hurts. 'Don't swear in this house! You stop saying your foul language to me, I won't have it. Don't swear!' and I'm hanging on to the edge of the sink to stop from falling over, I'm going dizzy. It makes me ill to hear bad words said before God and he knows it and he says it all the more, over and over, and my hand's under the tap and my head's swimming and ringing loud and the water turns red.

That night, I mend the door lock with one hand, while my other hand is throbbing through the cloth, and I hear him hammering and sawing in the shed in the yard, like it's been for days now into the night, but I don't care any more about what he's doing, I don't care, and I don't care if God doesn't want me to say it, I wish he were dead. I wish he were dead.

Serious Money *by Caryl Churchill*

The 'serious money' of the title refers to the fortunes to be made and lost working in the City on the Stock Exchange. Scilla's brother, a suspected insider dealer, has been murdered and she is attempting to find who the murderer is – though not for any reason of filial affection. The play is written as a modern verse play in which every character's over-riding passion is for money. This is a direct monologue to the audience.

Scilla   So Zac went back to Corman and I thought I'd better go to work despite Jake being dead because Chicago comes in at one twenty and I hate to miss it. I work on the floor of LIFFE, the London International Financial Futures Exchange.

Trading options and futures look tricky if you don't understand it.
But if you're good at market timing you can make out like a bandit.
  (It's the most fun I've had since playing cops and robbers with
  Jake when we were children.)
A simple way of looking at futures is take a commodity,
Coffee, cocoa, sugar, zinc, pork bellies, copper, aluminium, oil –
  I always think pork bellies is an oddity.
  (They could just as well have a future in chicken wings.)
Suppose you're a coffee trader and there's a drought in Brazil like
  last year or suppose there's a good harvest, either way you might
  lose out.
So you can buy a futures contract that works in the opposite direction
  so you're covered against loss, and that's what futures are basically
  about.
But of course you don't have to take delivery of anything at all.
You can buy and sell futures contracts without any danger of ending
  up with ten tons of pork bellies in the hall.

On the floor of LIFFE the commodity is money.
You can buy and sell money, you can buy and sell absence of money,
    debt, which used to strike me as funny.

For some it's hedging, for most it's speculation.
In New York they've just introduced a futures contract in inflation.
    (Pity it's not Bolivian inflation, which hit forty thousand per cent.)

I was terrified when I started because there aren't many girls and
    they line up to watch you walk,
And every time I opened my mouth I felt self-conscious because of
    the way I talk.
I found O'levels weren't much use, the best qualified people are street
    traders.
But I love it because it's like playing a cross between roulette and
    space invaders.

Pond Life *by Richard Cameron*

Pogo is eighteen years old and mentally ill. She lives at home with her parents and has a single friend, Trevor, who makes cassette tapes of music which calm Pogo down. On one particular night Trevor and his friends go to the local ponds to fish for a giant carp. Trevor has left a tape for Pogo telling her that he's leaving their home town.

In this speech Pogo is visiting Trevor when she starts to be plagued by the 'voices' which trouble her.

Pogo Half a pound of tuppeny rice
Half a pound of treacle
Mix them up and make them nice
Pop goes the weazle

She comes into the shed and begins mixing the fish bait.

A stir for luck, a spit for luck. (*Spits in bowl.*) Hubble bubble toil and trouble. Pint of maggots, jar of worms, cat food, dog food, fish food, elephant's poop, bull's blood. Mix me a match, catch me a catch. Walk three times backwards round it and then you'll see the fish you're going to marry. [. . .] (*Frightened.*) Trevor, hurry up and come back with the stuff. I don't want to be on my own.

(*Singing.*) I won't let the sun go down on me I won't let the sun go down.

(*Getting distressed.*) 'There's nothing you can't do if you put your mind to it', as my old grandad used to say.

Did he?

I don't know, I never had a grandad, I was making it up.

Aye, well, there's nowt so queer as folk, is there?

You're bloody queer. You're mental.

'If tha ever does owt for nowt, allus do it for thysen.'

(*Singing through tears.*) There's nothing you can do that can't be done
There's nothing you can sing that can't be sung.
There's nothing you can say
But you can learn how to play the game
it's easy
All you need is love . . .

You're mental. You're barmy. (*Singing.*) Pogo is a nut case, you're a
fruit and nut case.

You're brain's dissolving. It's turning to slush. Your head's a slush
puppy machine.

I don't want you. You're not getting in. I won't let you get in. I'm
thinking of . . . I'm thinking of . . . [. . .] You wet the bed.

Don't tell anybody. Please don't tell anybody.

You piss yourself. You can't even control your own bladder.

(*Very fast.*) I'm trying. I'm trying to be . . . I'm trying to keep afloat.
Floats. Delicate little floats. Precious. It's always in my box. It's not
there for catching fish.

It's the glorious sixteenth today, Pogo, let's go down to the lake and
fish for tench. We'll try the lift method. It's deadly for bottom
feeders like the noble tench. You put a worm on and I'll try bread.

Look, my float's moving!

Wait. Strike!

It's on. Wow! It's going like a train.

Looks like worm is the bait today.

Oh, Trevor, I'm losing it. Hurry up. I'm losing my thoughts. It's
going to snap the line. It's getting away.

'Stopping By Woods On A Snowy Evening' by Robert Frost.

Whose woods these are I think—

I want to throw up, talking about poems, you fat pig.

The woods are lovely, dark and deep,
But I have promises to keep
And miles to go before I sleep
And miles to go before—

I put you to sleep like a pig shot with a bolt through the head.

Confusions *by Alan Ayckbourn*

Beryl is one of five characters who are all enjoying a solitary afternoon in the same park. They become involved in an unwitting game of musical chairs – each hoping to avoid enforced contact with one another by changing benches. Beryl has just moved from her bench and starts explaining to the stranger next to her why.

Beryl (*sitting*) Thanks. Sorry, only the man over there won't stop talking. I wanted to read this in peace. I couldn't concentrate. He just kept going on and on about collections or something. I normally don't mind too much, only if you get a letter like this, you need all your concentration. You can't have people talking in your ear – especially when you're trying to decipher writing like this. He must have been stoned out of his mind when he wrote it. It wouldn't be unusual. Look at it. He wants me to come back. Some hopes. To him. He's sorry, he didn't mean to do what he did, he won't do it again I promise, etc., etc. I seem to have heard that before. It's not the first time, I can tell you. And there's no excuse for it, is there? Violence. I mean, what am I supposed to do? Keep going back to that? Every time he loses his temper he . . . I mean, there's no excuse. A fracture, you know. It was nearly a compound fracture. That's what they told me.

Indicating her head.

Right here. You can practically see it to this day. Two X-rays. I said to him when I got home, I said, 'You bastard, you know what you did to my head?' He just stands there. The way he does. 'Sorry,' he says, 'I'm ever so sorry.' I told him. I said, 'You're a bastard, that's what you are. A right, uncontrolled, violent, bad-tempered bastard.' You know what he said? He says, 'You call me a bastard again and I'll smash your stupid face in.' That's what he says. I mean, you can't have a rational, civilized discussion with a man like that, can you? He's a right bastard. My friend Jenny, she says, 'You're a looney, leave him for God's sake. You're a looney.' Who needs that? You tell me one person who needs that? Only where do you go? I mean, there's all my things – my personal things. All my – everything. He's even got my bloody Post Office book. I'll finish up back there, you wait and see. I must be out of my tiny mind. Eh. Sometimes I just want to jump down a deep hole and forget it. Only I know that bastard'll be waiting at the bottom. Waiting to thump the life out of me. Eh?

The Gift *by Roy Williams*

Jamaica. Janet and her mother, Heather, return to Jamaica from London in order to bury Janet's brother, Andrew. Heather is grief-stricken at the loss of her son but Janet is more conflicted – torn between love for her brother and exasperation at the dual standards her mother displays towards them both.

In this speech Janet is talking at the graveside. The spirit of Andy has returned from the dead and Janet is talking animatedly to him . . .

Janet (*laughing*) No! No it was yu! Don't lie Andy. I distracted Mum, yu were the one who unscrewed the top of the salt bottle, and I dared yu to, cos it was my turn to dare yu remember? Shame! The look on her face, remember that? I thought she was gonna croak man. The salt went all over her chips. And as usual she looked at me like I was the one who did it. Like butter wouldn't melt in yer mouth. You were her favourite, you know yu were. Who she give the belt to? Thank yu. (*Mocks.*) Yu got licks, yu got shit. I'm jus' stating a fact thass all. (*Aside.*) Virgin! Sorry. (*Aside.*) Short arse. Yer dead and yu still can't take a joke. Andy hold up, hold up man. I wanna ask yu summin? Can I, yu know, touch yu?

Janet *reaches out for her brother's hand.*

Janet Am I doing it, am I touchin' yer? Oh man this is weird. Yu know yu really scared me the oder day yu bastard. Yu tryin' to kill me or wat, yu want me lined up next to yu or summin? Why me? Why not Mum? She loves yu, she doesn't love me. (*She listens.*) I can't tell her that. I can't tell her that. It was your fault. Kiss my arse, I aint doin' it. Wat chance? Wat bloody chance could I have wid her?

Find Me *by Olwen Wymark*

Jean is the mother of Verity, an unbalanced child who is not actually retarded – therefore there is no definable place for her within the medical or social services. The family are left to cope with Verity's increasingly difficult behaviour on their own.

Jean has just been denied help by the social services. The social worker assures her that they all feel she is 'managing wonderfully well'.

Jean What are we going to do? Dear God, what are we going to do? Managing! Perhaps it would be better for all of us if we couldn't manage. Then they'd have to do something. Maybe if I became an alcoholic . . . I could. My God, I think I could sometimes.

Pause.

When I go next door to Suzanne's some nights and we sit and get a bit tight together on whisky and talk about all sorts of things and laugh – just for a little while I can forget. The thoughts stop going round and round in my head. The relief of just feeling like an ordinary person. The relief. Supposing when Miss Everitt Social Services came round today she'd found me dead drunk on the floor. 'Dear me, Mrs Taylor, you're not managing wonderfully well today.'

Pause.

Imagine your own child driving you to drink. Your own child that you love.

Pause.

I don't even know if I do love her. I don't know what I feel. Pity – oh, pity for her. Why did it have to happen? Poor Verity. Poor, poor baby.

Pause.

But fear too. She seems to like to frighten me – enjoys it. She never does it to Edward. I really think sometimes she hates me. And he's so good to her – so patient and kind. All those holidays he takes her on. He doesn't talk much about them afterwards but I know, I know she crucifies him. And I feel mean and cowardly because I didn't go too.

Pause.

And guilty. Did I do it? Was it my fault? When I was pregnant with her – all those weeks when she was inside me I thought she was so safe. Nothing could hurt her and yet all the time. . . . Was it me? Did I – contaminate her? Oh God. . . .

She stops herself.

She was so beautiful when she was a baby. Even now sometimes when you look at her when she's asleep. When I'm out with her sometimes I wish she was ugly. Deformed or crippled. Something people could *see*. Then they would pity her too. Instead of getting nervous and embarrassed and moving away from us as if we were lepers. Oh God, will nobody help us? Can't anybody help us?

Shopping and Fucking *by Mark Ravenhill*

Lulu works with her friend Robbie selling telephone sex. Both she and Robbie live in a world where relationships are reduced to commercial transactions and capitalism is the defining characteristic of a cynical society.

In this speech Lulu has returned home spattered with blood. She tells Robbie what has happened . . .

Lulu I mean, what kind of planet is this when you can't even buy a bar of chocolate? [. . .] [I was] walking past the Seven-Eleven and I think: I'd like a bar of chocolate. So I go in but I can't decide which one. There's so much choice. Too much. Which I think they do deliberately. I'm only partly aware – and really why should I be any more aware? – that an argument is forming at the counter. A bloke. Dirty, pissy sort of— [. . .] Wino sort of bloke is having a go at this girl, young— [. . .] Student girl behind the counter. Wino is raising his voice to student.

There's a couple of us in there. Me – chocolate. Somebody else – TV guides. (Because now of course they've made the choice on TV guides so fucking difficult as well.) And wino's shouting: You've given me twenty. I asked for a packet of ten and you've given me twenty.

And I didn't see anything. Like the blade or anything. But I suppose he must have hit her artery. Because there was blood everywhere. [. . .] And he's stabbing away and me and TV guide we both just walked out of there and carried on walking. And I can't help thinking: why did we do that?

Road *by Jim Cartwright*

Road is an episodic play set in a derelict street in Lancashire where unemployment and despair are rife. Throughout the play different characters reveal the state of their lives.

Clare is the young girlfriend of Joey. He sees no point in living and has retreated to bed where he intends to starve himself to death. Clare joins him, not really understanding the purpose of the protest, but determined to stay with him. The speech is a response to his question: 'Why are you here anyway?'

———————————

Clare I don't know. I suppose I don't know what else to do. Every day's the same now. You were my only hobby really, now you're out of it, seems mad to carry on, all me ambition's gone. I filled in a *Honey* quiz last week. 'Have you got driving force?' I got top marks all round. But where can I drive it, Joe? I lost my lovely little job. My office job. I bloody loved going in there you know. Well you do know, I told you about it every night. I felt so sweet and neat in there. Making order out of things. Being skilful. Tackling an awkward situation here and there. The boss smiling at me, telling me I was a good worker. Feeling the lovely light touch of morning when I went out to work. To have a destination. The bus stop, then the office, then the work on the desk, the day's tiny challenge. I mean tiny compared to proper big company work. But I loved it. Exercise to my body, my imagination, my general knowledge. Learning life's little steps. Now I'm saggy from tip to toe. Every day's like swimming in ache. I can't stand wearing the same clothes again and again. Re-hemming, stitching, I'm sick with it, Joe. I'm the bottom of the barrel. I must be. How many letters have I writ? A bloody book's worth, and only ten replies, each the same really. Seven bleeding photo-bleeding-copied. I heard my mum cry again last night. My room's cold. I can't buy my favourite shampoo. Everybody's poor and sickly-white. Oh Joe! Joe! Joe!

Ten Tiny Fingers, Nine Tiny Toes *by Sue Townsend*

England, the future. Society has now been divided into different classes with various rules and strictures. Only the upper classes are allowed to breed and the lower classes, of which Section 5 is the lowest, are treated like peasants, live in poverty and are forbidden the right to read, write or even have children. In this society anyone who is no longer financially valuable, e.g. the elderly, people with disabilities etc. is put to death by euthanasia.

In this speech the Orderly, who works as a midwife in the genetically enhanced breeding centre, is concerned that her own elderly mother will not willingly undergo euthanasia.

Orderly I keep thinking it's Friday. I'm off this weekend, going to see my mum, she's only got five months to go. Three days, five months. She's being difficult though, she says they'll have to come and get her, she won't do it herself. I'm hoping she'll change her mind, it could reflect badly on me. She doesn't see why she should have to go at all. She says she's fit and well and good for another twenty years. She says she's invincible. The invincible woman. I've said to her, 'What's the point of living on after seventy years? You're not working, you're not generating wealth, your brain will go, your body will fall apart. It's unpatriotic. You'll be a parasite.' She's still living in the old days when people died all over the place – on holiday, in the car, in shops. It was inconvenient and it caused a lot of disruption. People having days off work for funerals and rushing about with death certificates. I said, 'Mum you're being selfish – it's a tiny injection and then a long sleep. You deserve it, you've worked hard' – but she wouldn't listen. I hope she'll be in, she sometimes goes off at the weekends – painting with an easel she found on a rubbish tip. She walks miles with this easel thing under her arm. She's a terrible embarrassment to me. And you know what she paints? The countryside! (*She laughs.*) Don't ask me why. She's got all these little *pictures* up on the walls in her room. It's a sign of senility. I mean there are professionals whose job it is to paint pictures. *She* doesn't need to do it. I'm surprised she's got away with it for so long. And now this stubborn attitude she's taking towards Death Day. (*Determined.*) Well she'll have to go along with it. I've booked a day off for it and I can't go chopping and changing – it's on the computer now, so that's final. It'll be a relief for me when she's gone. I can concentrate on work. At the moment I'm a bag of nerves, wondering what the daft old bat will do next. If it gets out about the pictures . . .

Whale Music *by Anthony Minghella*

Whale Music is a play based on the interaction of women
with one another – the pregnant Caroline providing the
central point around which they pivot.

Stella is a warm, exuberant but cynical woman who
rarely lowers her defensive barriers. In this speech she
explains to Caroline the reason for her behaviour at the
dance the night before.

Stella They do exist, Caroline. It's not my imagination. There's something I do, have done before. If I land a really three-star macho man . . . you know, the whole image . . . never stops telling you what a great time he's going to give you. He's going to make you really cry out, you know, like drowning . . . and all this whispered or licked at you across his MG or yelled in your face on his Yamaha, a great gob full of, whatever, garlic, or grease or fag smoke, and fucking Brut – always Brut or Prick or Stud or Come or whatever they can dream up to call that very unpleasant smell that hides that other very unpleasant smell which is the smell of them getting turned on to you – and they want to get it up through your tights in some car park so that they don't have to cope with you afterwards, you know, because they have no feeling, nothing . . . dead eyes, dead bodies. So what I do is this. I give him . . . Mr Godsgift . . . I give him the real Penthouse cliché, right. Lick my lips, touch myself, scream a bit, play scared when he steps out of his knickers, I mean – awestruck – and I get so very excited in the first number. I always try and break things in his bedroom – preferably something expensive – because I'm so wild for it – and I give out all the words. And I can get it done in a few minutes and, well, there he is, slack-jawed, grinning, notching me up on the barrel, three-quarters asleep. So I leave him for a few minutes, then kiss him like it was love – and then I get going on him for round two. Well! Bit of a laugh, bit nervous now, Mr Godsgift, bit sheepish . . . but I'm good, OK, and he gets some response and it's going to be a great story for his pals in the morning: 'You should have seen this slag – she couldn't get enough of it!' And he makes ride number two, sometimes makes ride number three, perhaps, but he's losing and he's worried and he's sore and he's fucking terrified, and the NEXT time I make certain he falls apart. I'm surprised. I'm very disappointed he can't make it. I even get angry with him. And then I get dressed and come home and stand under the shower and scrub him off and if I could stand boiling water I'd boil myself clean to the marrow.

Five Kinds of Silence *by Shelagh Stephenson*

Mary is the abused wife of Billy, a violent and terrifying
man, who has been sexually abusing his entire family for
years. The play begins with the manslaughter of Billy by his
two daughters who have been driven to this violent act by
the abuse they have endured. Mary has tried to protect her
girls but has failed.

At this point in the play Mary has been taken into
custody by the police for questioning. She's attempted to
take the blame for the death herself but the police have
dismissed this. A sympathetic officer is curious to discover
what has actually been going on in the household. Mary
begins to describe her first experience of bereavement.

Mary I'm six years old, walking home from school. There's deep snow crunching on the ground and my feet are tingling cold. I have on wellingtons and green woollen mittens threaded through my sleeves with elastic. I get to my street, and before I can get to our house Auntie Ruby comes out of it in a black fur hat, and hurries me away. Oh the mite, she says, oh the mite. In my head it muddles with Almighty God whose son suffered and died because He loved us. Imagine the nails, Mary. Imagine the nails, Sister Bridget says, being driven into Our Lord's beautiful hands. Think of the pain, Mary, think of the blood, as the nail is driven through sinew and bone and soft, soft flesh. He suffered this because he loved us so much. I'm thinking this all the way to Auntie Ruby's. I'm thinking let the dark thing not happen, I will dwell upon the suffering of Our Lord, I will drive nails into my own hands only let it not happen. Ruby's house is dark and cold and something terrible is wrong, the praying didn't work. My food congeals on the plate, my heart is lodged in my throat like a stone. Why can't I go home, but I know the world has ended. Your poor mother. Your poor mother, is what they say. That chop will be put in front of you at every meal until you eat it. But my throat is closed. I will never eat again. Days pass, there are carols on the wireless, I feed the chop to the dog and my mother is not coming back. They've put her in the ground, they say. But won't she be cold? How will she breathe? How will she eat? Won't she be lonely? It is Christmas, and my poor mother is deep in the ground, up by the moor. I go back to my home. No point lighting a fire, says my father. We won't be having a tree. On Christmas Day I sit hunched in my coat, longing for my mother to come up out of the lonely cold ground, watching my father drink a bottle of whisky. I am mad with grief, he says, forgive me. I don't know what grief is but I start to cry anyway. I cry louder and louder but my mother never comes and my father doesn't wake. Through the wall, I can hear the neighbours having a sing-song.

Touched *by Stephen Lowe*

Sandra is one of a group of women, living in Nottingham, whose husband is still away fighting in the Pacific War. The play is set in the 100 days between V.E. and V.J. days.

Sandra informs her family that she is pregnant, but refuses to reveal the name of the father. This leads to a huge family row. The speech takes place after they have all left the house, leaving Sandra alone.

Sandra I took a picnic. What I could scrape together. Bread. My ration of cheese. Flask of tea. I took it all nice. Lace tablecloth. I stood, looking through the barbed wire. I walked off when they came out. Bent shouldered men in a crisp March. March. March. I marched off at a good pace. He was right behind me. Perhaps he spoke. I don't know. I had to find a certain place, that I must have found before, but I was still surprised when we came upon it. I must have found it earlier, but I couldn't believe it there, that I had looked for it, that I was returning to this place. I thought the ground is hard and dry. It won't stain my tablecloth, won't stain my dress. This is fine, anything can happen here, in the lace of these trees, and it won't stain. I knelt, and began to unpack my bag. I knew I could walk away and it may never have happened. I laid out the lace cloth, wiped out the creases, set out the flask, the food, around the edges like for a child's party. I stood and walked carefully around the outside of the edge. I looked up. I faced him. We stood apart. It suddenly was a very hot day. I felt faint. I thought, I'll fall. Look at him, I thought, look at him. He began to speak. His voice rose. Anger? Hate? I couldn't understand what he was saying. The crispness was going. The fog was settling in. His voice grew louder. He was undoing his clothing. His trousers. I knew what he was saying. He was giving me orders. He was . . . giving me . . . orders. I looked at him, and I knew the lace was there, the food was there. I

looked at him. I waited. Slowly his voice faded away. He stood
there, unbuttoned, sad, clumsy against the lace, like a puppet with
the strings broken. I spoke. I think they were the first words I spoke,
and the last bar one. You – I pointed to him – PRISONER. He looked
away. Frowned. Frowned like a little child. He understood me. It
hurt me. NO, I said. I shook my head, meaning no. He looked up. I
crossed the white to him. I put out my hands to him. I reached into
his crumpled clothes, I touched him. Touched. I felt the shiver. The
pulse. He is real. I . . . he . . . we are both here. The roughness of his
clothes, the softness of the man's skin. I want to go down in front of
him. I want him to go down in front of me. I want things I've never
dreamed of, sins I have always feared. I pray. A second's prayer. Not
to ask, Lord, but to thank. I want to be free, and I am free. I am real.
I am alive. The Lord is my shepherd. I shall not want. He maketh
me to lie down in green pastures: he leadeth me beside the still
waters. Thou preparest a table before me in the presence of thine
enemies; my cup runneth over. Lord. Holy mother. Holy child. The
Rainbow. The Rainbow.

The Wild at Heart Club *by Jenny McLeod*

Angie, an aspiring stand-up comic, and her friends all hang out together in the local club, known as the Wild at Heart Club. Although no one is actually officially part of a gang it is clear that they have certain loyalties and affiliations to one another. Angie is going out with Howie, a local 'gang' leader. The owner of the Wild at Heart Club, Risley, is having an affair with Angie. She thinks he genuinely loves her but he's actually using her as a means of entrapping and murdering Howie. Angie is desperate to escape the grinding poverty of her life and has a dream of going to Edinburgh and winning the Perrier Award, thereby achieving fame and fortune. She is also manipulating Risley by using his club as the jumping-off ground for her imminent Edinburgh triumph.

In this speech Angie is polishing her act for the last time before going to Edinburgh in front of punters at the Club.

Angie Yeah, I'm seventeen! (*All-round clapping.*) I'm glad I'm seventeen. Who'd want to be younger? To go through those seventeen years again? Been there! Done that! Do not want to do it again! Your fist kiss! I stood there thinking. 'Why's this guy putting his spit into my freshly Mcleaned mouth?' I felt like saying, 'If I'm thirsty I've got enough for a can of coke, thank you.' Please! Please! The first time you jump from your bedroom window to go to that forbidden rave, and you realise that that is not the reason they're called flower beds. I broke my right leg. Laid there till morning, knowing if I woke my ma, she'd know what to do with the left one. The milkman found me. He looks at me. In the flower bed. Laying flat out, holding my sodding leg, in mega-pain, and he looks at me. He says, 'A note would've been enough.' (*Enthusiastic laughter and clapping.*) Spoken by Angie Saunders, words by Brill Tyler.

Angie *points over to* **Brill**. **Brill** *is shy when the applause is directed to her.*

(*pointing at* **Brill**) Yeah she's the one! She's the one who sticks that hundred-watt bulb up my arse and shoves me out here. If you don't like what I've said tonight, blame her. As you know, this is the last show at the wonderful Wild at Heart Club. (*All-round groans.*) Don't we just love the Wild at Heart Club? (*Enthusiastic clapping.*) Owned by the wonderful Mr Risley. (*All-round groans.*) No, be good. Without Mr Adam Risley, the Angie Brill show wouldn't be off to the Edinburgh Fringe Festival tomorrow. (*Enthusiastic clapping.*) Where we'll be a great hit. Win the Perrier Award, transfer to a West End venue, get signed up for our own TV show, earn a million and retire before we're thirty! (*Cheers and clapping.*)

Fen *by Caryl Churchill*

Fen follows the lives of the women who work the potato harvest in the Fenlands. Margaret is a middle-aged woman, attending a Baptist meeting. Although this is the only time her character appears in the play, it is important to read the whole piece to understand the structure of the Fenland society.

She has been called upon to share the experiences which have led to her conversion to Christ.

Margaret I thought I would be nervous but I'm not. Because Jesus is giving me strength to speak. I don't know where to begin because I've been unhappy as long as I can remember. My mother and father were unhappy too. I think my grandparents were unhappy. My father was a violent man. You'd hear my mother, you'd say, 'Are you all right, mum?' But that's a long time ago. I wasn't very lucky in my marriage. So after that I was on my own except I had my little girl. Some of you knew her. But for those of you who didn't, she couldn't see. I thought at first that was why she couldn't learn things but it turned out to be in her head as well. But I taught her to walk, they said she wouldn't but she did. She slept in my bed, she wouldn't let me turn away from her, she'd put her hand on my face. It was after she died I started drinking, which has been my greatest sin and brought misery to myself and to those who love me. I betrayed them again and again by saying I would give it up, but the drink would have me hiding a little away. But my loving sisters in Christ stood beside me. I thought if God wants me he'll give me a sign, because I couldn't believe he really would want someone as terrible as me. I thought if I hear two words today, one beginning with M for Margaret, my name, and with one J for Jesus, close together, then I'll know how close I am to him. And that very afternoon I was at Mavis's house and her little boy was having his tea, and he said, 'More jam, mum.' So that was how close Jesus was to me, right inside my heart. That was when I decided to be baptised. But I slid back and had a drink again and the next day I was in despair. I thought God can't want me, nobody can want me. And a thrush got into my kitchen. I thought if that bird can fly out, I can fly out of my pain. I stood there and I watched, I didn't open another window, there was just the one window open. The poor bird beat and beat around the room, the tears were running down my face. And at last it found the window and went straight out into the air. I cried tears of joy because I knew Jesus would save me. So I went to Malcolm and said baptise me now because I'm ready. I want to give myself over completely to God so there's nothing else of me left, and then the pain will be gone and I'll be saved. Without the love of my sisters I would never have got through.